Outside My Window

Program Authors
Richard L. Allington
Camille L. Z. Blachowicz
Ronald L. Cramer
Patricia M. Cunningham
G. Yvonne Pérez
Constance Frazier Robinson
Sam Leaton Sebesta
Richard G. Smith
Robert J. Tierney

Instructional Consultant
John C. Manning

Program Consultants
Jesús Cortez
Robert E. Slavin

Critic Readers
Elaine K. Cannon
Linda Hassett
Sister Carleen Reck
Norma Rodríguez
Jane Sasaki
Michael M. Sheridan

**Scott, Foresman
and Company**

Editorial Offices:
Glenview, Illinois

Regional Offices:
Sunnyvale, California
Tucker, Georgia
Glenview, Illinois
Oakland, New Jersey
Dallas, Texas

Scott, Foresman Reading: An American Tradition   Gold Medal Printing

Acknowledgments

Text
"A House Is a House for Me" by Mary Ann Hoberman, from *A House Is a House for Me.* Copyright © 1978 by Mary Ann Hoberman. Reprinted by Permission of Viking Penguin Inc.

"Who Has Seen the Wind?" by Christina Rossetti. From *Sing-Song.* The Macmillan Company, Copyright © 1924.

Artists
Reading Warm-up: Blanche Sims, 6–13
Section 1: Andrea Eberbach, 41–48, 69; Barbara Lanza, 14–15; Dick Martin, 50; Steve Schindler, 16–32, Bernard Wiseman, 51–59, 69; Richard Walz, 60–66, 68, 69
Section 2: Dick Smolinski, 90–98, 105, 125; Lydia Halverson, 124; Ann Iosa, 114–121, 123, 125; Barbara Lanza, 70–71; Dick Martin, 106–113, 125; Elizabeth Miles, 80–89, 125; Margaret Sanfilippo, 72–79, 125
Section 3: Nan Brooks, 144, 181; Marlene Ekman, 168–179, 180; Lydia Halverson, 136–143, 180; Yoshi Miyake, 182–189; Nancy Munger, 167; Ed Taber, 146; Lane Yerkes, 156–164, 166, 180

Freelance Photography
Dean Abramson, 33–34, 36–40, 69; James Ballard, 145, 147–155, 180 (right); Ryan Roessler, 99–104, 125, 126–127

Photographs
Page 35: Dean Abramson; Pages 128–129: W. Perry Conway, TOM STACK & ASSOCIATES; Pages 130, 132, 133 (bottom), 134, 135, 180 (left): Robert & Linda Mitchell; Page 133 (top): Tom Myers; Page 131: © M. Lynelle Sachen/Hillstrom Stock Photo; Page 49: Terry Qing/FPG

Cover Artist
Elizabeth Miles

ISBN: 0-673-74403-5

Copyright © 1989, 1987

Scott, Foresman and Company, Glenview, Illinois.
All Rights Reserved. Printed in the United States of America.

78910—VHJ—969594939291

Contents

A Game for Kim

by Nancy Ross Ryan

Kim is not happy.

Kim wants to play.

She wants to have fun.

Kim looks at Dave.
She wants him to play.

Dave says, "I can't play.
I am painting."

Painting looks like fun.
Kim says, "I can help."

The ball falls into the paint.
The ball is green.

Dave says, "What a mess!
I do not want your help.
Take your ball and go."

Kim says, "This is not fun."

Kim picks up the ball.

She takes the ball to the fan.

The fan looks like fun.

She says, "The fan may help
my green ball."

The paint gets on Mr. Brown.

Mr. Brown is green.

Mr. Brown says, "Look at this!

What a mess!

Take your ball and go."

Kim says, "This is not fun."

Kim says, "I want to have fun.
Painting is not fun.
The fan is not fun.
What can I do?"

Kim sees a ball game.

Kim says, "May I play with you?"

The boy says, "You may play.
Your green ball looks good.
Give it to me.
We can play with it."

Kim says, "This will be fun!"

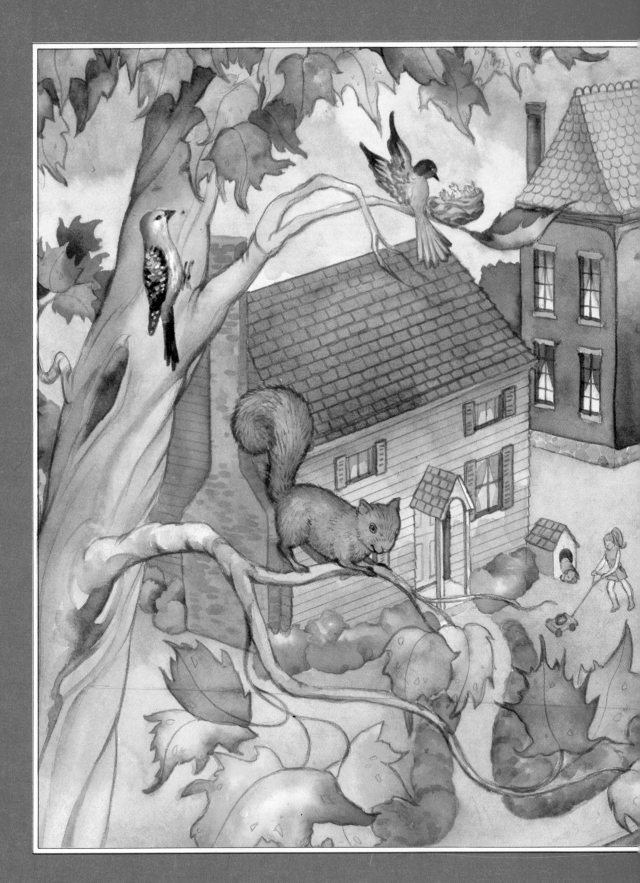

1

At Home

You and I have homes.
Animals have homes.
You will see homes in
this book.

A Good Home

by Mary Hynes-Berry

Furry said, "I will look for a home.
I do not want a big home.
I will not pick a noisy home.
I want a good home for a
squirrel like me."

Furry went up a tree.
Furry looked into a little opening.

"I like this," Furry said.
"It is little.
 It is not noisy.
 This is a good home for a squirrel
 like me."

Ginger was looking for a home.
She went to the tree Furry picked.
Ginger looked up and down.
She said, "This looks like a good
home for me."

She put her bag into the tree.

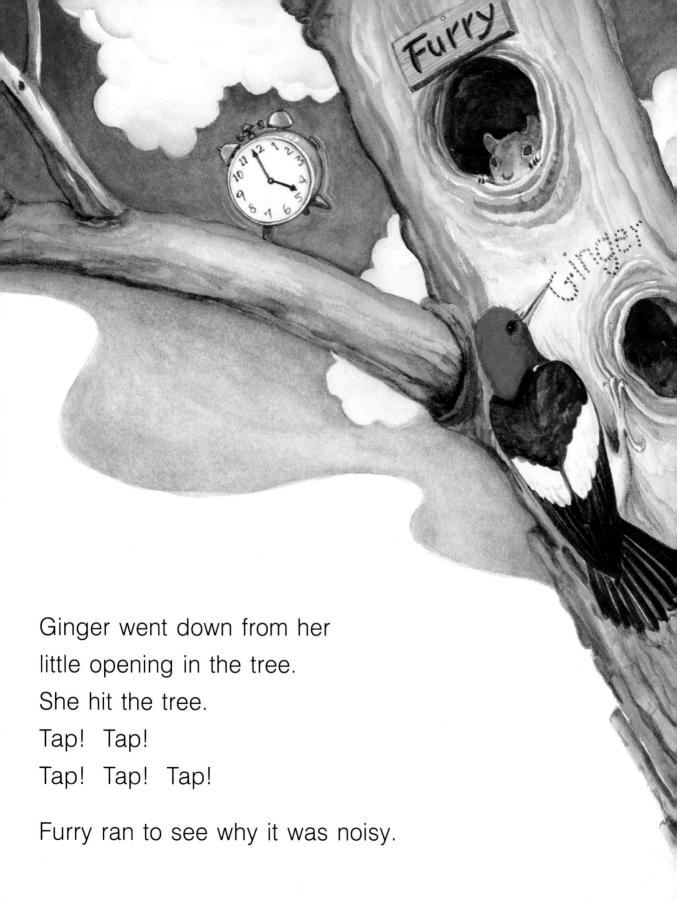

Ginger went down from her
little opening in the tree.
She hit the tree.
Tap! Tap!
Tap! Tap! Tap!

Furry ran to see why it was noisy.

"This is not good," Furry said.
"Get down!
Go!
This is a good home for a squirrel.
You are not a squirrel.
A noisy animal can't
share my tree."

"It is not yours," said Ginger.

"This tree is my home.

I can do what I want.

I want to do this."

Ginger hit the tree.

Tap! Tap!

Tap! Tap! Tap!

"Get down from my tree!" said Furry.

Slinky looked on.
"I think you and Ginger are
noisy animals," she said.
Why can't you share this
big home?"

"I will tell you why," said Furry.
"Ginger hits the tree.
She is noisy.
And she makes the clock fall down.
The clock can't get me up."

Slinky said, "Why not have Ginger
help you?
Ginger can tap the tree to get
you up.
Ginger will be your clock.
You and Ginger will get what you want.
You can share this good home."

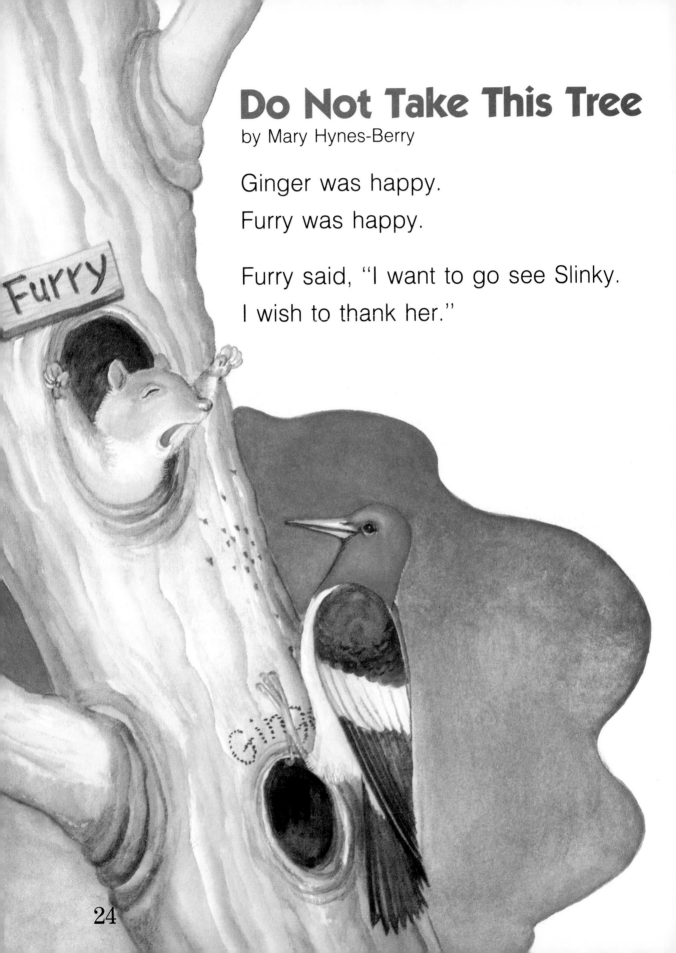

Do Not Take This Tree

by Mary Hynes-Berry

Ginger was happy.
Furry was happy.

Furry said, "I want to go see Slinky.
I wish to thank her."

24

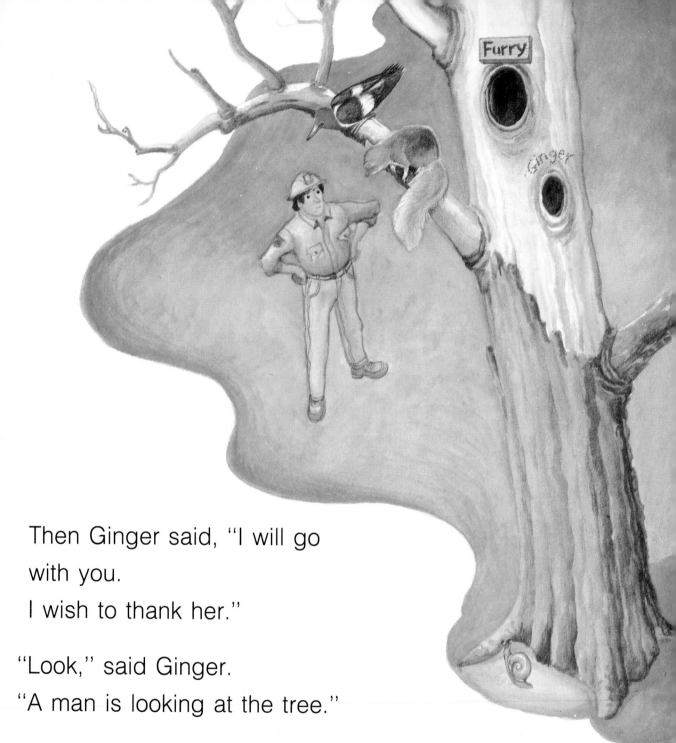

Then Ginger said, "I will go
with you.
I wish to thank her."

"Look," said Ginger.
"A man is looking at the tree."

"This tree is sick," said the man.
"I will have to chop it down."
The man went to get help.

Both Furry and Ginger went to see Slinky.

"Come," Furry said.
"A man may chop down the tree."

"Why?" said Slinky.

"The man said it is sick,"
said Furry.
"This is bad, and I am sad.
I do not want him to take my
little home."

Ginger was mad.

She looked at her home.

She said, "It is such a good home.

Furry and I both are happy.

The man can't chop it down!

I will tell him not to.

The man can read what I have to say."

Tap! Tap!
Tap! Tap! Tap!

Furry wanted to help.
Then Slinky wanted to help.

"Both you and I can share the paint,"
said Furry.

"Look!" said the man.
"It says, 'Do not chop this
tree down.'"

Ginger was looking at the man.
Furry was looking at the man.
Slinky was looking at the man.

"Look at the little animals.
I think the animals painted this,"
said the man.

"I think the squirrel and the bird
share the tree.
Animals can have homes in sick trees.
I will not chop it down,"
the man said.

"Thank you for such good thinking,"
said Furry to Ginger.

"Thank you for such good help,"
said Ginger.

"I wish to thank the man," Ginger said.
Then she hit the tree.
Tap! Tap!
Tap! Tap! Tap!

1. What is Furry looking for?
2. Why is Furry mad at Ginger?
3. The man will not chop down the tree. Why not?
• 4. What are cats, pigs, and squirrels?
   trees   animals   homes

• Comprehension: Class relationships

Talk

Tell a boy and a girl why you like the animal homes.

Speaking/Listening: Discussion

Come See My Home

by Joanne Bernstein

Do you see this big **lighthouse?**

I live here with my family.

My home is not like your home.

From my bed, I do not see trees.

From my bed, I see water.

The water and the lighthouse
are noisy.

The lighthouse helps boats.
The man in this boat did not see
where to go.
The man looked at the lighthouse.
The lighthouse helped the man.
From the lighthouse, my family sent
him home.

Boats help my family.

What my family wants is sent in

a boat.

This boat sent a box for my family.

This boat sent what my family eats.

This boat sent books for me.

It's fun to go up into the lighthouse.
Birds live up here.
It's fun to look down.
The boats look little from here.

Boys and girls do not live here
with me.
Trees do not live here.
Squirrels do not live here.

At first, I wished for boys and
girls to play with.
At first, I wished for trees and
squirrels to look at.

I play with the birds.
I play with my family.
I look at the water and the flowers.
The birds, my family, the water,
and the flowers make me happy.

My home is not like your home.

It's big.

It's noisy.

It's fun.

My home is a lighthouse.

The Three Little Pigs

a folk tale adapted by Joanne Bernstein

The three little pigs wanted to leave home.

Fred said, "I'll go to make a house."

Gus said, "I'll go with you."

Al said, "I'll go with you."

The three little pigs went to make three houses.

First, Fred looked for straw.

"May I have your straw?" Fred said to a man.

"I'll make a straw house."

Fred put up a house first and went to bed.

Next, Gus looked for sticks.

"May I have your sticks?" Gus said to a man.

"I'll make a stick house."

Gus put up a house and went to bed.

Next, Al looked for bricks.

"May I have your bricks?" Al said
to a man.

"I'll make a brick house."

Al put up a house and went to bed.

A wolf looked at the first house.
It was the straw house.
"Little pig, little pig, let me come in!" the wolf said.

"Not by the hair of my chinny, chin, chin," said Fred.

"Then I'll blow your straw house down!" said the wolf.
And the wolf did.

Fred ran to the next house.

Next, the wolf looked at the
stick house.

"Little pigs, little pigs, let me
come in!" the wolf said.

"Not by the hair of my
chinny, chin, chin," said Gus.

"Then I'll blow your stick house
down!" said the wolf.
And the wolf did.

Fred and Gus ran to the next house.

Next, the wolf looked at the
brick house.
"Little pigs, little pigs, let me
come in!" the wolf said.

"Not by the hair of my
chinny, chin, chin," said Al.

"Then, I'll blow your brick house
down!" said the wolf.
The wolf did blow and blow.
The brick house did not blow down.

"I'll come in," the wolf said.

"You will see!"

The pigs put water on to get the wolf.

The wolf went down into the house.

The wolf looked at the water and ran.

The three happy little pigs did a jig.

Comprehension Check

Think and Discuss

1. What is it like to live in a lighthouse?

• **2.** Put **water, boat,** and **house** in ABC order.

3. Why can't the wolf blow down the brick house?

4. What do the pigs do to make the wolf leave?

• **5.** Put **Gus, Fred,** and **Al** in ABC order.

• Study Skill: Alphabetical order

Communication Workshop

Write

Do you like houses? Draw the house you like. Write and tell why you like the house.

Writing Fluency: Sentence

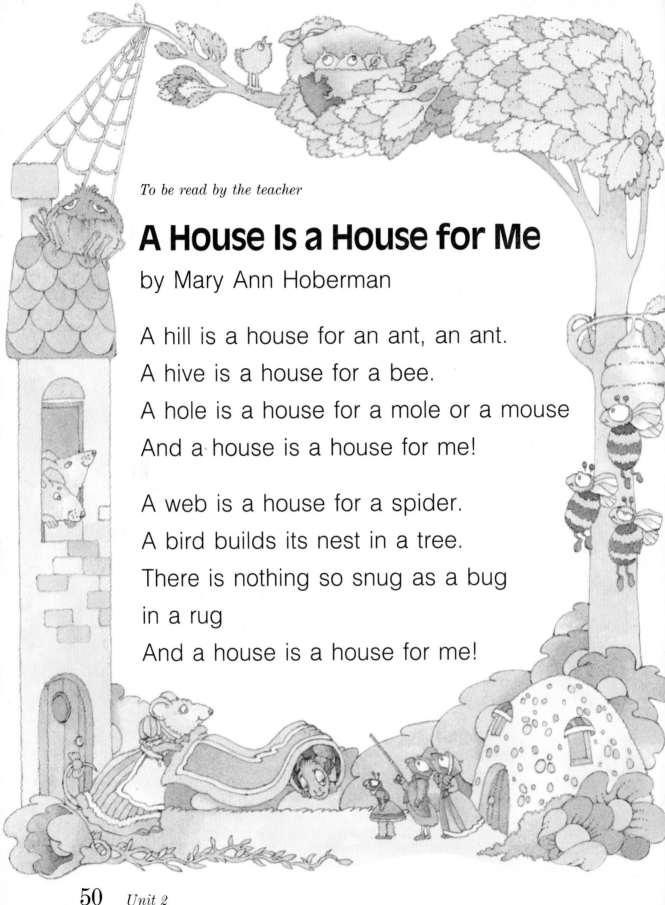

To be read by the teacher

A House Is a House for Me

by Mary Ann Hoberman

A hill is a house for an ant, an ant.
A hive is a house for a bee.
A hole is a house for a mole or a mouse
And a house is a house for me!

A web is a house for a spider.
A bird builds its nest in a tree.
There is nothing so snug as a bug
in a rug
And a house is a house for me!

The Tree House Home

by Bernard Wiseman

"Mom," said Bob. "Pat and Kim want to
move into the tree house with Jane
and me."

Kim said, "May we go and live in the tree house with Bob and Jane?"

Mom said, "You may. When will it happen? When will you move?"

"When we get water," said Pat.
"We have food to eat."

"Here's water," said Mom.
"You can move into the tree house."

"Come on!" said Jane. "This is a big
day! The day we move into the
tree house!"

"Come on, Kim!" said Jane.
"Get up here. I don't want my friend
to be last!"

Kim smiled. "I will not be last.
Look! Bob will be last."

"I will not let it happen!" said Bob.
"My friend Pat will be last."

Pat said, "Your friend Pat is last."

"Jane," said Bob, "Go down and get
books. With no books you'll cry.
Kim, you go down and get games. With
no games to play you'll cry."

"Bob," said Jane, "come down with me
and get paints and brushes. With no
paints and brushes you'll cry."

Pat said, "I will come down and get
flowers. Flowers will give the house
a happy look."

Kim said, "Jane, get pads to write on.
I can't call my Mom from the tree.
She's at home. I will write to her."

Pat said, "I will write to my Mom.
She's in the house, and I can't
call her from the tree."

"I can call my Mom," said Jane. "Mom!
Mom! Will you get more books for me?"

Kim said, "Here comes your Mom.
She's got more books."

Jane said, "We've got what we want.
Let's go live in the tree house."

"We CAN'T!" said Bob. "Don't you see?
We can't get in the tree house, and
the food is up in the tree house."

Kim said, "Why did this have to happen? What a sad day. What a mess! I think I'll cry."

Mom smiled and said, "Don't cry. Your tree house is little. You can't move into it, but you can eat. We can make a big pizza."

Pat and Bob and Kim and Jane smiled.

Good Day, Spider

by Caron Lee Cohen

Sara looked at Bird and Dog.

"Good day, Bird and Dog," she said.

Spider looked on.

"Sara did not see me," Spider said.

"She says 'good day' to Bird and Dog.

She does not say 'good day' to me."

"She's not my friend," said Spider.

Spider was sad.

"I'll move closer to Sara.

I'll ask Bird if I can live with him.

If I move down there, Sara will see me.

Then she will say 'good day' to me."

The next day, Spider jumped a <u>slow</u>
jump down to Bird.
Spider looked like a falling feather.

"May I move in?" Spider asked Bird.
"I want to move closer to Sara.
  I want her to see me."

"You may," Bird said.
"<u>But</u> you are little and slow.
  Sara may not see you here."

Sara looked at Bird and Dog.
"Good day, Bird and Dog," she said.

Spider looked on.
"But Sara did not see me, Bird,"
   Spider said.

"Move closer to her," said Bird.
"If you move to where Dog lives,
   you'll be closer.
   Sara will see you there."

63

The next day, Spider jumped a slow
jump down to Dog.
"May I move in?" Spider asked.

"You may," Dog said.

Sara looked at Bird and Dog.
"Good day, Bird and Dog," she said.

Spider was crying.
"This was my last move, Dog.
What can I do to have Sara see
me?" Spider asked.

Dog smiled.

"There, there, don't cry," Dog said.

"You'll have to move closer.
  Why not live on Sara's boat?"
  asked Dog.

"Good thinking, Dog!" said Spider.

"But I am slow.
  Can you help me get there?"

"I'll blow you there, slow Spider,"
  said Dog.

Zap!

Spider was on the boat.

Sara looked up and smiled.
"Good day, Spider," she said.

"Good day, my friend Sara,"
    Spider said.

Meet a Reader

Sylvia Jimenez is a first grader
from California.

Sylvia likes to read all the time, so
her mother gets her lots of books!

Sylvia likes books about zoo animals.
Her favorite book is Too Many Monkeys
with pictures by Kelly Ocehsli.

What else does Sylvia like to read?
"I like to read books about little
people, like me," she says.

When Sylvia is not reading, she likes
to play with her friends.

Comprehension Check

Think and Discuss

• 1. What happens first, next, and last?
   a. The tree house is a mess.
   b. The friends will make a pizza.
   c. The friends move to the tree hous
• 2. What happens first, next, and last?
   a. Spider moves to Bird's home.
   b. Sara says "good day" to Spider.
   c. Spider moves to the boat next to Sara's bed.

• Comprehension: Time Sequence

Communication Workshop

Talk

Tell a friend what you can do to help your family if you move.

Speaking/Listening: Cooperative learning

LOOKING BACK

Thinking About What You've Read

Where do the animals live?

Where do the boy and girl live?

What do you like about the homes?

Write about you and the homes you like.

2

Trees, Water, and Wind

Do you like to sit under a tree?
Do you like to swim in the water?
Do you like to play in the wind?

You will see what fun trees, water, and wind can be.

Under the Flowering Tree

by Caron Lee Cohen

Ted was under a flowering tree.
The wind was blowing.

"The wind makes music when it blows.
I want to make music!
I wish I had a recorder!" Ted said.

"Mrs. Jones makes recorders to sell.
I can't pay for one, but I'll go
see her.
I'll ask her if I can help her.
She may let me pay for a recorder
with my help," said Ted.

Ted said, "I want a recorder, but I
can't pay for one.
May I please help you here?
I'll help you for days and days to pay
you for a recorder.
I want to make music like the wind."

Mrs. Jones looked at Ted.

"You may help me.

You can help me find good wood.

If you find good wood, I'll give you a recorder," she said.

Ted was happy.

Ted and Mrs. Jones went to find wood.

"Will you please tell me what you do
to make recorders?" asked Ted.

"The first step is to get the wood,"
said Mrs. Jones.
"Please don't take wood from
live trees.
Please pick up wood that is not on trees."

"Is this stick a good one?" asked Ted.

"I can make a good recorder from this
stick," said Mrs. Jones.

Mrs. Jones and Ted went under the
flowering tree.

"The next step is to cut the wood,"
said Mrs. Jones.
"I cut openings in the wood.
I'll cut the stick you picked up.
This step takes three days.
You go home.
I'll meet you here in three days."

Ted went home.
Mrs. Jones cut and cut.

In three days, Ted went to the
flowering tree.

"Please sit down," said Mrs. Jones.
"I'll tell you the last step.
The last step is to make the
wood smooth.
A smooth recorder looks good.
A smooth recorder makes good music.
You can smooth this recorder.
I'll help you," she said.

Ted smoothed the wood.

"You can't pay for a recorder, but you
helped me find good wood.
You picked the stick for this
recorder and smoothed it.
For your help, you may have it," said
Mrs. Jones.

At last, Ted had a recorder.
"I can make music!" said Ted.

Under the flowering tree, Ted played
the recorder.
Ted played music with the wind.

The Little Tree

by Caron Lee Cohen

One day Dan and Fran played under a
little tree.

Fran saw seeds on the ground.
"Look at the seeds!" she said.
"We can eat the seeds.
We can take the seeds home!
This tree is a real friend."

The squirrels picked up seeds and
went home.

One day, when Fran and Dan played
under the tree, Dan said, "We can tell
a story under this tree.
I will make up a story.
I will tell my story to you."

"This tree is a real friend,"
said Fran.

The squirrels had fun telling a story
and went home.

One day, when Fran and Dan played
under the tree, Fran said, "We can
dance under this tree.
The wind is blowing music in
the leaves.
We will dance and dance."

"This tree is a real friend,"
said Dan.

The squirrels did a squirrel dance and
went home.

One day, when Fran and Dan played
under the tree, Dan said, "We can
sleep on the ground under this tree.
The leaves make a good bed.
We can sleep and sleep."

"This tree is a real friend,"
said Fran.

The squirrels had a good sleep and
went home.

Then, one day when Fran and Dan
went to the tree, it was on the ground.

"We had such fun under this tree!
How did this happen to my real
friend?" asked Dan.

"A tree can fall down if it is hit,"
said Fran.

"I am sad," said Dan.

Fran said, "Find a seed from the tree.
We will make a tree come up
right here.
Next fall, the tree will be little.
But next fall we can tell a story,
dance, and sleep here."

"How?" asked Dan.

"Here is how," said Fran.

1. Find a seed.

2. Dig in the ground.

3. Put in the seed.

4. Water the seed.

Here is how Fran and Dan's tree looked.

Comprehension Check

Think and Discuss

1. What does Ted want? Why?
2. Why can't Ted pay for a recorder?
- 3. To make a tree come up, what do you do first, next, then, and last?
    a. Dig in the ground.
    b. Water the ground.
    c. Put a seed in the ground.
    d. Find a seed.

- Comprehension: Steps in a process

Communication Workshop

Write

What can you do with a seed?
Write what you do first, next, and last.

Writing Fluency: Using order words

Fun in the City

by Marjorie and Mitchell Sharmat

"Why do we live in the city?" I asked
Mom one day.

"The city can be fun," said Mom.

"Fun?" I said. "How can we have fun?"

"We are not working today," said Mom.
"The sun is up, and the sky is blue.
This is a good day for fun."

Dad put on his jacket and cap.

"Where are we going?" I asked.

"You'll see," Dad said.

"I have my jacket," I said.

Mom said, "So do I. Let's go!"

We jumped into the car.
When I looked up, I saw
boats and ships on the river.

We left the car, and Dad went to get
a boat.

"Put on your jacket, Pete," Mom said.
"When we get in the boat, the wind
may be blowing."

Dad called and we ran and jumped into
the boat.

We went down the river and looked
at the city.

"Look, Pete! There is where Mom
and I work," said Dad.

"Why do you like to live and work in
the city?" I asked.

"It's so close to the river," he
said. "We like to look at the boats
and water."

The sun went away, and the water looked green and mad.

"Here comes the wind," Mom said.

The wind blew and blew. It blew water into the boat.
It blew water on Dad and Mom and me.

"What if the boat tips?" I asked.

"The boat will not tip," Dad said.

"We will float to the lighthouse."

We floated to the lighthouse.

"Look, Dad," I said. "I see a man."

"We are so happy to see you," Dad called to the man. "We saw your lighthouse from the river. The wind blew water into the boat, and we floated here," he said.

"Come into my house," said the man. "Don't be sad. The wind will go away."

"First we will eat. Then I will
let you see a working lighthouse.
Do you like fish? I have good fish
to eat."

I smiled and said, "I like fish."

His fish was good!
Then we looked at his lighthouse.
Dad looked at the sky.

He said, "Look! There's the sun
and the blue sky. We can leave."

We left the lighthouse, went into the
boat, and up the river.
I saw a boat painted like a car.
I saw more ships and boats pass.
The ships were big, but the boats
were little.

"This boat looks so little," I said.
"It may be little, but it's a good
boat. The wind and water did not make
it tip. There's the city!" I said.

Dad smiled. "I am happy to see the city," he said.

"I like the city," I said. "It's next to the river. This day on the river was fun."

We left the boat, went to the car, and then went home.
What a good day in the city!

Boating

CONTENT-AREA READING

by Pat Demuth

Being in a boat is fun.

But when you go in a boat, think about safety.

Come with me.

I'll share my safety tips with you.

Think about your safety.

First, put on this jacket.

This jacket can float.

The jacket floats, so you will float

if you have one on.

Go boating with friends and family.
I go boating with my mom.
She can swim.
If I fall into the water, she can
help me.

Take a safety kit with you.
If you get a cut, the kit can
help you.
Look at what is in this kit.
You can see what to put in yours.

Be a friend to the river.

Keep the river clean.

Keep the river clean so you will have clean water to look at.

Keep the river clean so the fish will have a clean home.

Think about safety when you
go boating.
Think about keeping the river clean.
Then you, your family, and the fish
will have fun!

Think and Discuss

1. Why do Pete and his family go to the river?

• 2. What happened when the wind blew and blew?

3. What safety tips did you read about in "Boating"?

• 4. Why is it good to keep a river clean?

• Comprehension: Cause and effect

Communication Workshop

Talk

Make up a story about going on a boat. Tell a friend what you see and do.

Speaking/Listening: Cooperative learning

The Wind and the Sun

a fable by Aesop
adapted by Betty von Glahn

CLASSIC

"Sun!" called the wind.
"Sun, come play with me."

The sun opened his eyes.

"Let's play a game," said the wind.

"Let's not," said the sun.
"I want to sleep now."

The wind did not like that.

"A good sun does not sleep when he
is working.
You are a bad sun," said the wind.

The sun's eyes opened and he said,
"I am not!"

"Let's see how good a sun you are,"
said the wind.
"We will play a game to make that boy
take off his jacket."

"All right, Wind.
But it's your game.
You go first," said the sun.

The wind blew.
A big cloud blew in.
Then the wind blew again.
The boy's red hat blew off.

"How about that?" asked the wind.

"The little boy did not take off
his jacket," said the hot sun.

Then the wind blew again and again.
Now the boy's balloon blew into
a tree.

"How about that?" asked the wind.

"That is not bad, but the boy has his
jacket on," said the hot sun.

"My," said the boy.
"I have a chill!"

"Do you see that?" asked the sun.
"The boy is chilled.
He will not take that jacket off now."

"I give up," said the wind.
"Let's see if you can do it."

The hot sun reached down to the boy
on the ground.
The clouds floated off.
The sky was blue again.

"I am hot now," said the boy.
"I think I'll take off my jacket."

And he did.
Then he got the balloon.

"That was a trick!" said the wind.

"It was not a trick," said the
hot sun.
"You worked and worked.
But you sent big clouds and
chilling winds.
The boy did not take off his
jacket.
I did not have to work like you did.
I sent a little sun to him.

The boy did take his jacket off.
You see, Wind, I am a good sun."

"I can see that," said the wind.

"Now let's be friends again.
But first I will sleep,"
said the sun.

The wind smiled.

Up in the Sky

by Betty von Glahn

This is a story about Duck, Bear,
Fox, and Mrs. Green's balloon.

One day Mrs. Green went to see Duck.
"Would you fly my balloon from my
home to the river?" she asked.
"I want to see if it can fly."

"I would like that!" said Duck.
"I think my friends would like to fly
with me.
I'll go to their homes right now."

First, Duck went to tell Bear.

Bear was so happy that she jumped
up and down.

"I'll fly like a bird," said Bear.
I'll fly to the top of the clouds!"

Then Duck and Bear went to tell Fox.

Fox was so happy he did a dance.

"I would like to fly to the top of
the clouds!" said Fox.
"Into the sky we will fly and fly!"

On the big day, all of the city went
to Mrs. Green's house.
Dogs and cats ran about.
Moms and dads sat on the ground.
Boys and girls were playing.

Then the balloon went up.
All eyes looked to the sky.

In the balloon, up in the clouds, all
eyes were looking down.

"Don't you like flying?" asked Duck.
"I think this balloon is fun."

Bear and Fox were not happy.

"I don't think I like flying at all,"
said Bear.

"I want to go home," said Fox.

"We are going to hit the top
of that tree!" called Fox.

The balloon brushed the tree's top.

With that, Bear and Fox ran
under a box.

It was hot under the box.
But Duck's friends were not
about to move.
Their eyes did not open again.

At last, their balloon passed the
river and floated to the ground.

"We are here!" said Duck.

Bear and Fox opened their eyes.
Mrs. Green and all of her friends
were there.
Mrs. Green said, "You are tops!"

Then she asked, "Did you have fun?"

Duck said, "I did!"

"I would not call it fun," said Fox.

Bear smiled and said, "That is right!
Let's leave flying to the birds.
The sky is their home."

Meet a Reader

France Joseph is a first grader from Illinois.

France likes animals, so she likes to read books about animals.
She also likes to read books about different people.
She likes to read because "It's fun and sometimes I read some very interesting things," she says.

France likes to read at the library. That's because she's read all the books she's got at home!

Besides reading, France likes to do math and play games on a computer. She also likes to draw her favorite animal, the African elephant.

Comprehension Check

Think and
Discuss

1. The boy does not take off his jacket when the wind blows. Why?

• 2. The boy has a hat on.
The wind blows it off.
What does the wind blow off?

• 3. The balloon passed the river.
It floated to the ground.
What floated to the ground?

• Comprehension: Word referants

Communication Workshop

Write

Draw about a day when the wind blew and blew. Have a friend ask about your drawing. Write down what your friend asks.

Writing Fluency: Questions

To be read by the teacher

Who Has Seen the Wind?

by Christina Rossetti

Who has seen the wind?
Neither I nor you:
But when the leaves hang trembling
The wind is passing thro'.

Who has seen the wind?
Neither you nor I:
But when the trees bow their heads
The wind is passing by.

LOOKING BACK

Thinking About What You've Read

Tell about what you read.
Pick one story you like.

Write and tell a friend what you
like about that story.

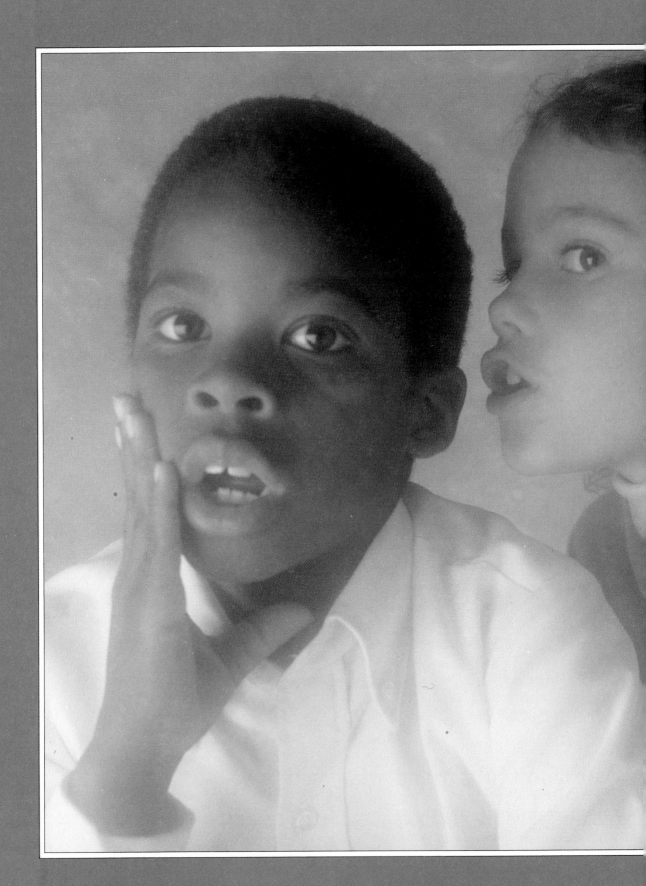

3

Tell Me a Secret

Do you have many
secrets?
Keeping a secret can
be fun.

You will read about
secrets.
Think about what
happens.

 # A Secret in the Ground

by Betty von Glahn

You may have to crawl to get into it.

There is no light in it.

Many animals that live in it can't see at all.

What is it?

It's a **cave.**

A cave can be under the ground where you play.

A cave can be under a city.

A cave can be a secret if no one finds the opening to it.

Caves are in the ground, so the sun
does not reach into caves.
There is no light at all in a cave.
If your mom were right next to you,
you could not see her.
Trees and flowers can't grow if there
is no light.
So trees and flowers don't grow
in caves.

This bug has to have light to live
and grow.
Many bugs and animals have to have
light to live and grow.
So many bugs and animals can't live
in caves.
But some can.
Let's take a look at some cave bugs
and cave animals.

There are many bugs that live and
crawl in caves.
Some cave bugs are light
in color.
Some are white.
With so little color, they could not
live under the hot sun.
So a cave is a good home.

Do you see the **cave fish?**
They don't see you.
They have no eyes at all.
But eyes are of little help in a cave.
There is no light so eyes could not
help the fish see.

Here is a **cave crab.**
Like the cave fish,
it can't see.

A **bat** likes to sleep in a cave.
Many bats that live in caves eat the
cave bugs you saw.
Some bats leave the cave to eat.
They eat bugs that live and grow in
the light.
They eat fruit that lives and grows
in the light.

There are many caves that no one
can find.
There are many caves that no one can
get into.
So the bugs and animals in caves live
secret lives.
Caves can keep good secrets!

Where Is My Bear?

by Betty von Glahn

I have a purple bear.

My mom gave it to me when I was three.

When I play, my purple bear plays
with me.

When I sleep, my purple bear sleeps
with me.

When I am not with my bear, I keep him
in a very secret house.

One day, when I went to the secret house, my bear was not there!

"Mom, I can't find the purple bear you gave me," I called.

"Where do you keep him, Son?" my mom asked.

I could not tell her.
"I can't tell you, but the purple bear you gave me is not there!" I said.

My mom and I looked for my bear all day, but we could not find him.
I was very sad.

Then I said to my mom, "My purple bear likes fruit.
I'll put some fruit on top of his house and my bear may come home."

"All right, Son," said my mom.
"But I don't think purple bears like fruit very well, Son," she said.

I put some fruit on top of the
secret house.
Princess, my dog, sniffed at
the fruit.

The next day, the fruit was not on the secret house!

"Mom, Mom!" I called.
"My purple bear was here but he left. He likes the fruit I gave him!"

"What, Son?" my mom asked.
"Your bear likes the fruit you gave him?"
She looked at Princess.

That day, I played ball with Princess.

"Here Princess," I said.
"Bring the ball to me.
Bring it here."

Princess ran with the ball to
her house.

"No, Princess, bring it here!" I called.

I ran to Princess.

Princess crawled into her house.

Then she crawled out.

She did not bring the ball with her.

I looked into the house for the ball.

"Mom, Mom," I called.

"Here's what is left of the fruit
and here's my purple bear!"

I crawled into the house and got
my purple bear.

"So you ran off with my bear and the
fruit," I said to Princess.

"Bring your bear here and I'll clean
him, Son," said my mom.
"It looks like both you and Princess
keep secrets in houses," she said.

But my house was not a secret to
Princess.
Now her house is not a secret
to me!

Think and Discuss

• **1.** What is "A Secret in the Ground" all about?

    a. flowers

    b. caves

    c. animals

• **2.** What is "Where Is My Bear?" all about?

    a. a boy looking for his bear

    b. a dog called Princess

    c. a boy in a secret house

• Comprehension: Main idea

Communication Workshop

Write

Think about a cave under ground. Tell your friends what you see in your cave.

Speaking/Listening: Cooperative learning

Make a House from a Box

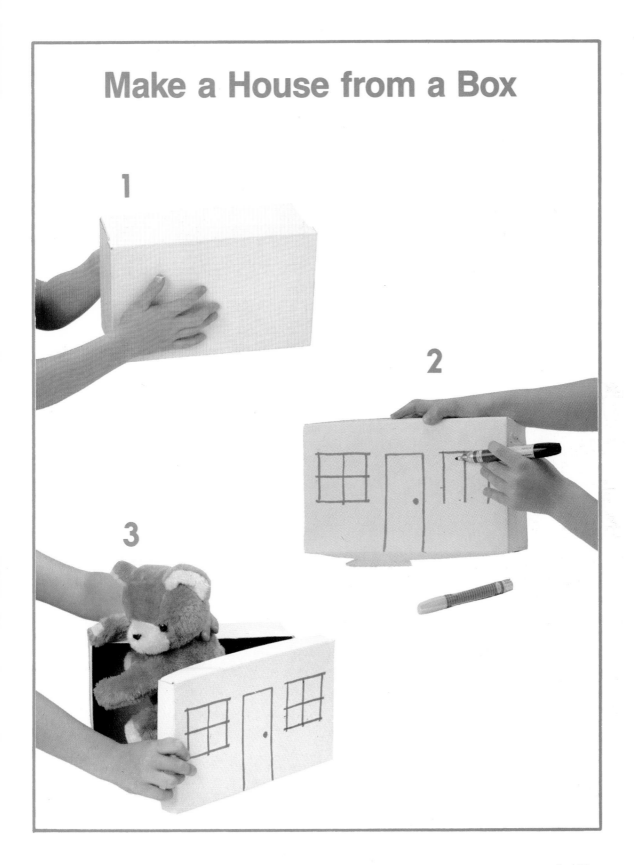

My Secret Friend

by Caron Lee Cohen

BOYS: I have a secret
That I will not keep.
My secret is a secret friend.
He meets me when I sleep.

GIRLS: When I go to sleep, you see,
My friend (he is called Red),
Comes and does a dance for me
Right next to my bed!

ALL: My mom and dad are sleeping
So they can not see
The very secret fun we have—
My secret friend and me!

A Box for Mrs. Lee

by Liane Onish

In this play are:

WENDY

TIM

LUIS

JAN

PAUL

MRS. LEE

JOAN

(The children in MRS. LEE's class

are playing.

WENDY has a box.

The box is shut.)

WENDY **(to TIM):** I have a secret in

this box.

I have to keep the box shut so

no one sees.

TIM: Tell me!

What is it?

May I see?

WENDY: You can't see.

I have to keep the box shut.

But I'll tell you.

I have new mittens and a hat in this box.

They are for Mrs. Lee.

Don't tell!

TIM: Who me?

I would not tell.

I can keep a secret.

(**TIM goes to LUIS, who is playing.**)

TIM (**to** LUIS): Do you see that box?

There is a secret in it, so Wendy

must keep it shut.

I can't tell you what it is.

LUIS: You always tell me your secrets!

TIM: If I tell you, you must not tell

the class.

LUIS: Oh no, I will not tell the class!

TIM: Wendy has new mittens in the box.

There are cats on the mittens!

(LUIS goes to JAN, who is reading.)

LUIS **(to JAN):** Do you see the box that
Wendy has?
There is a secret in it so she
must keep it shut.

JAN: What is it?
I can keep a secret!

LUIS **(with a laugh):** Wendy has her new
cat in the box!
The cat is called Mittens!

JAN **(laughing):** What a good secret!

(JAN goes to PAUL and JOAN, who are playing ball.)

What do you think will happen next?

PAUL and JOAN: We saw you laughing.

What is going on here?

JAN: There is a good secret.

It's about what is in Wendy's box.

JOAN: Oh, I like secrets!

Please tell Paul and me.

JAN: Wendy has her cat in the box.

The cat has on blue mittens!

MRS. LEE: Children come in now.
Come in and sit on the rug.

JOAN (to PAUL): Did Janet say Wendy
has blue kittens in the box?

PAUL: Can a kitten be blue?

**(The children go in and sit on
the rug.)**

MRS. LEE: Why are you children
laughing?

PAUL: Wendy has blue kittens in
the box!
Put the kittens on the rug so
we can see, Wendy!

JAN: No, that is not it!
Her cat is in the box.
The cat has blue <u>mittens</u> on.

LUIS: No, no, the cat in the box is

called Mittens.

It's a new cat.

TIM: No, there are new mittens in

the box.

There are cats on the mittens.

WENDY (laughing): No one is right!

I don't have blue kittens and I

don't have a new cat!

I have new mittens and a hat in

this box.

They are for you, Mrs. Lee.

(WENDY **gives the box to** MRS. LEE.

  MRS. LEE **sees the hat**

  and mittens

  She puts the hat and mittens on

  the rug.)

MRS. LEE: I don't want a kitten, but I
  do want a hat and mittens.
  Thank you, Wendy!

WENDY: I am so happy that you like
  what I had for you.
  The class helped to keep it a secret!

(All children laugh.)

Rob's Big Secret

by Liane Onish

Rob was a little rat who could not
find his home.
He had looked for many days when
Mrs. Mouse saw him.

She asked, "Can I help you?
You look very sad."

"I can't find my home and my family.
Where can I live?" he asked.

Mrs. Mouse said, "We can help you out.
We always help a mouse in need.
You must come live with Mr. Mouse
and me."

Rob said, "Thank you, but you see I
am not a . . . "

"Stop," said Mrs. Mouse.
"You don't need to thank me.
Come with me to your new home."

At first, Rob and his new family were very happy.

But Rob was not a mouse.

Rob was a rat.

He would grow to be very big.

He did not want to keep such a big secret, but he needed a home.

So he did not tell.

What do you think will happen?

"See how Rob eats!" said Mr. Mouse.
"He does not stop!"

"We always help a mouse in need,"
said Mrs. Mouse.

"Oh my," said Mr. Mouse.

Rob smiled, but did not tell
his secret.

"See how Rob sleeps!" said Mr. Mouse.
"He is so big he can't fit in his bed!
 He must sleep on the rug!"

"We always help a mouse in need," said
Mrs. Mouse.

"Oh my," said Mr. Mouse.

Rob smiled but did not tell his
secret.

One day, Rob was out in the woods.
He had fruit to eat all day.
When he wanted to come in, he could
not fit into the house.

"See how Rob looks now!" said
Mr. Mouse.

"We always help a mouse in need,
but Rob, you can't fit in the house!
We can't help you out there!" said
Mrs. Mouse.

"Oh my," said Mr. Mouse.

A rat saw what was happening.

"A mouse?" he asked Rob.

"Who, you?

You are a rat!"

Rob looked down.

"I could not tell you," he said to

Mrs. and Mr. Mouse.

"You always help a mouse in need.

I am not a mouse, but I needed help."

"Oh my," said Mr. Mouse.
"That was a very big secret.
   It isn't good to keep a secret
   like that."

   Rob was not happy about what he did.
"It was bad of me to keep that secret.
   You are mad.
   Can I make it up to you?
   I can get bags of fruit for you!"
   he said.

"That would be good, Rob," said
   Mr. Mouse.

"I'll go to find a new home now,"
said Rob.

"Why don't you come live with me?
You'll always fit into my house,"
said the rat.

"Will you come see me there?" Rob asked
Mrs. and Mr. Mouse.

"Yes, we will come to see you.
We are mad, but you will always be a
friend," said Mrs. Mouse.

"Oh my," said Mr. Mouse.

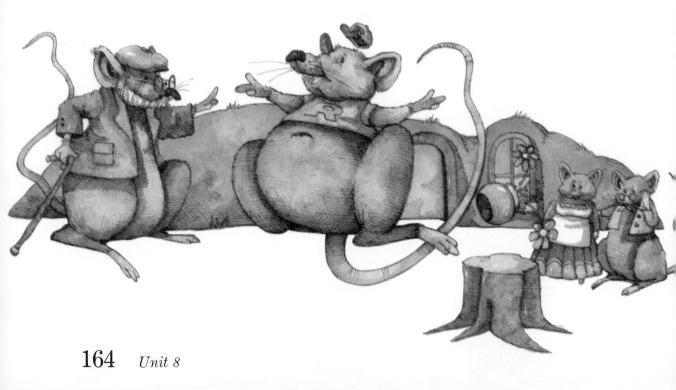

Meet a Reader

Andre Shepard is a first grader from Connecticut.

Andre likes to read books about people.
His favorite books are the <u>Mr. Bumba</u> books by Pearl A. Harwood.

Andre likes to read after he finishes his homework.
He reads at his desk in his bedroom.

When Andre is not reading, he likes to play with trucks and robot toys.

1. Wendy does not want the class to see what is in the box. Why?
2. Were you right about what Jan would do next?
   How could you tell?
3. Why does Rob keep his secret?
4. Were you right about what would happen to Rob?
   How could you tell?

Comprehension: Predicting outcomes

Communication Workshop

Write

Write your first and last names. Are they right? Show your name to a friend.

Writing Fluency: Capitalizing proper names

Look Now, My Friend

by Caron Lee Cohen

Look now, my friend!
There is a secret in the wind.

It floats down from the sky;
It can dance and it can fly.
It is white, and it can grow.
Look out to see the secret snow!

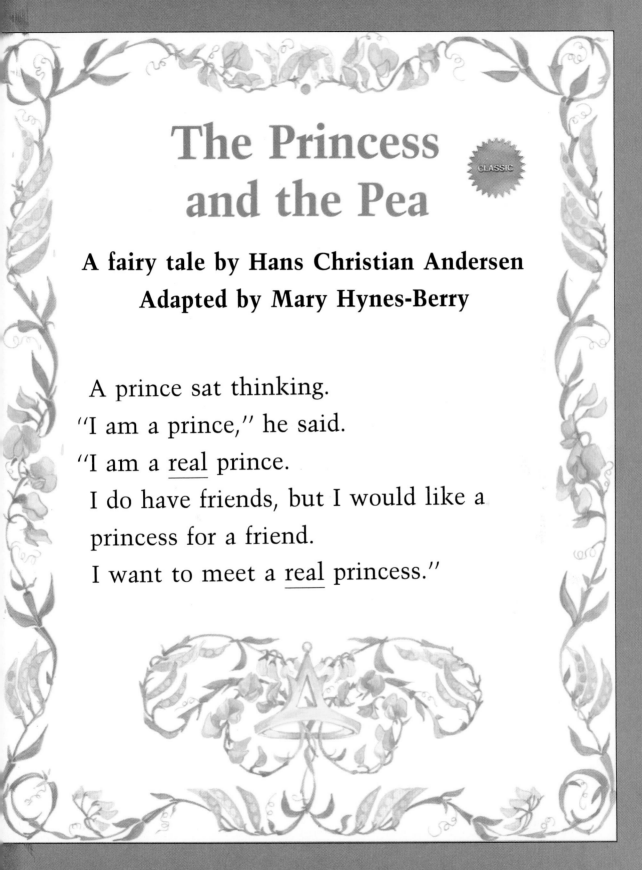

The Princess and the Pea

A fairy tale by Hans Christian Andersen

Adapted by Mary Hynes-Berry

A prince sat thinking.

"I am a prince," he said.

"I am a <u>real</u> prince.

I do have friends, but I would like a

princess for a friend.

I want to meet a <u>real</u> princess."

When the prince saw a girl, he would
ask, "Are you a princess?"

Some would say, "Why no!"
Some would say, "I don't think so."

The prince would look sad and say,
"Then I'll have to go on looking.
You see, I want to meet a real
princess."

One day the queen went to her son and
said, "Now then, Son, don't be sad.
Some day you'll meet a princess."

"When will I meet one?" the
prince asked.
"And how can I tell if she is <u>real</u>?"

"I can tell," the queen said.
"I will find out."

Then, one very bad day, a girl
happened to come to the prince's home.

"Please help me," she said.
"It is very bad out now.
I can't get home.
May I sleep here?
My family will thank you.
You see, I am a princess."

"You don't look like a princess,"
  said the prince.

"But I am a princess," said the girl.

"I can tell if you are a <u>real</u> one,"
  said the queen.
"Come in."

The queen went to make up a bed for the girl.

In secret she put one little pea on the bed.

Then she had some mattresses put on top.

"Get in," the queen said to the
  girl who said she was a princess.
"Tell me if the bed is right."

  The girl got in bed.
  Then she gave a cry.
"Oh!
  What is sticking me?" she asked.

"Let's put many, many mattresses on the
    bed," said the queen.
"That may help."

She had many, many mattresses put
    on top.

The next day, the girl said, "I could
not sleep at all.
What do you think was sticking me?"

The queen gave the girl the pea.
"This is why you could not sleep.
I put a pea under your mattresses
in secret.
You <u>are</u> a real princess.
No one but a real princess could tell
a pea was under that many mattresses."

"How happy I am!" said the prince.
"I have always wanted to meet a real
  princess!"

The princess smiled.
"I have always wanted to meet a real
  prince," she said.

From then on, they were very happy.

Thinking About What You've Read

The stories tell about secrets.
Tell what all the secrets are.

Write to a friend. Tell your
friend a secret.

Books to Read

In Our House
by Anne Rockwell

Read to find out why a family
likes their house.

Wake Up, Jeremiah
by Ronald Himler

See how the sun comes up to
bring a new day for Jeremiah.

The Cat in the Hat
by Dr. Seuss

Would you tell your mom if a cat
in a hat played in your home?

A a

animal Many animals live in the woods. **animals**

B b

balloon Jane's balloon floats in the sky. **balloons**

bug The bug is crawling on the ground. **bugs**

C c

car Matt is in the car with his mom. **cars**

class The class is reading now. **classes**

D d

dip Pam will dip the brush into the paint.

dog A dog can be a good friend. **dogs**

E e

eat Joe likes to eat chicken.

F f

fish Fish live in water.
Fish swim.

G g

game Tim and Sara are
playing a game. **games**

H h

house Val lives in a house.
houses

I i

into The squirrel puts seeds into the tree.

J j

jig A jig is a dance.
The boys and girls are doing a jig. **jigs**

K k

kitten A kitten grows up to be a cat. **kittens**

L l

little The flower is very little.

185

mouse

pond

M m

mouse A mouse is a little animal.

N n

new Pat has a new jacket.

O o

on The cat is sleeping on the rug.

P p

pond A pond is a good home for ducks. **ponds**

186

Q q

queen The queen is about to eat. **queens**

R r

read Rob likes to read books about animals.

recorder The girl blows into the recorder to make music. **recorders**

S s

snow Snow falls from the sky. Snow is white.

T t

tree The tree has many green leaves. **trees**

tub Wendy cleans her dog in a tub. **tubs**

U u

under The bug is under a stick.

V v

van Ted's family is getting into the van. **vans**

W w

wolf The wolf runs in the woods.

Y y

yellow Yellow is a color.
The can has yellow paint in it.

Z z

zap Zap! The light went on
and off.

zebra The zebra is eating straw.
zebras

The words listed below are listed by unit. Following each word is the page of first appearance of the word.

Looking Ahead

home   15
animal 15

Unit 1

noisy 16
squirrel 16
went 17
tree 17
little 17
was 18
down 18
her 18
hit 19
why 19
share 20
clock 22
wish 24
thank 24
then 25
man 25
chop 25

bad 26
both 26
mad 27
such 27

Unit 2

lighthouse 33
live 33
family 33
bed 34
water 34
boat 35
did 35
sent 35
it's 37
first 38
three 41
I'll 41
house 41
straw 42
next 43
stick 43

brick 44
wolf 45
let 45
blow 45
jig 48

Unit 3

move 51
we 52
when 52
happen 52
food 52
day 53
don't 54
friend 54
last 54
smiled 55
you'll 56
cry 56
write 57
call 57
she's 57